Y0-EDP-599

Where We Live

France c^2

Donna Bailey and Anna Sproule

STECK-VAUGHN
L I B R A R Y
A Division of Steck-Vaughn Company

Hello! My name is Simone.

I live in Brittany in northwest France.

I am wearing my traditional costume.

The cap on my head is made of lace.

My home is in Saint-Malo.

Saint-Malo is by the sea.

The old part of the city has a big wall around it.

Can you see the wall in the picture?

3

My home is inside the old city.

From my bedroom window,

I can see over the city wall to the sea.

Many tourists come to Saint-Malo
in the summer.
People like to swim and picnic on the sandy beaches.

Saint-Malo is a good place for sailing.
There is a large harbor for big yachts.

Smaller boats dock at the big marina.
People enjoy sailing in the bays.

In Brittany, sailors must watch the tides.
The tide goes out so far at Saint-Malo
that many boats are left
leaning over on their sides.

When the tide is low, my family
often goes looking for sea snails and
clams in the wet sand.

People who live in Brittany are called Bretons.

Many Bretons are sailors and fishers.

There are many fishing boats

in the harbor at Saint-Malo.

The fishing boats go out early every morning
to catch fish in the English Channel.
The fishers use nets to catch the fish.

The fishing nets often get holes in them.
When the boats return to harbor,
the fishers must mend their nets.

The fishers sell their morning catch
in the fish market.
The people of Brittany eat a lot of fresh fish.

Some fishers use lobster pots
to catch lobsters.
This man has a lobster pot.

Farther around the coast at Cancale,
the fishers grow oysters in
oyster beds.

Cancale oysters are sent to markets
all over France.
This man is selling oysters at
a stand in Paris.

People in France celebrate festival days
with special dinners and activities.
They buy their favorite foods in the market
to prepare traditional meals.
Many people attend holiday church services.

Some French markets are outdoors.
People come to this market
in Brittany to buy fruits,
vegetables, and fresh bread.

French bakers make bread in different shapes.

Each shape has a special name.

Baguettes are long, straight loaves.

Croissants are round, flaky rolls.

This baker gets up very early to bake the bread.
People in France buy fresh bread every day.
On festival days the baker is busy.
He makes many loaves for holiday dinners.

The people of Brittany have many traditions
and customs.
They speak their own language, as well
as French.
Many of the older women wear
traditional lace caps.

Brittany is famous for lace.
The women make mats and tablecloths,
as well as their own caps.
They often sell their lace from
stands by the road.

Girls in Brittany wear traditional dresses
on Sundays and for special festivals
called pardons.
A pardon is a church festival in honor
of one of the Breton saints.

The biggest pardon in Brittany is
the Festival of Cornouaille.
The festival takes place in the city of
Quimper during the last week in July.
People come from all over Brittany to see it.

The girls from different parts of Brittany
wear different kinds of hats made
from lace and linen.
The men also wear special costumes and hats.

Each part of Brittany has its own
traditional costume.
Some girls wear shawls over their shoulders.
Others wear aprons and lace collars.

One of the girls is chosen to be
the Festival Queen.
She will be Queen of Cornouaille
until next year's festival.

Dancing is an important part of
the Festival of Cornouaille.
People dance in parades and on a stage
in the main square of Quimper.

These men are playing Breton music
as they walk in a parade
through the streets.
One plays a horn, and the other plays
the Breton bagpipes.

Each region of Brittany tries to win
prizes in the competitions for
singing, dancing, and music.
These girls are singing the songs
of their region.

Each region also has its own special dances.
These dancers join hands in a circle and
stamp their feet as they dance.

Bands from all over France come
to play their drums and bagpipes.
Everyone enjoys the music and
fun of the Festival of Cornouaille.

Index

Reading Consultant: Diana Bentley
Editorial Consultant: Donna Bailey
Executive Editor: Elizabeth Strauss
Project Editor: Becky Ward

Picture research by Jennifer Garratt
Designed by Richard Garratt Design

Photographs
Cover: Ann Hughes Gilbey (Denis Hughes Gilbey)
Colorific Photo Library: 11 (Snowdon/Hoyer), 12 (Erich Spiegelhalter), 19 (Ronny Jacques), 20 (David Turner)
Douglas Dickens FRPS: title page, 6
Festival de Cournaille, Quimper, France: 24,25,27,29,31
French Government Tourist Office: 32
The Hutchison Library: 3,7,8,15 (Bernard Re'gent), 4,5 (Christine Pemberton), 16 (John Downman),
Ann Hughes Gilbey: 17 (Denis Hughes Gilbey), 18 (Lyn Gamble), 22 (Bernard Gerard), 2,23,28
Robert Harding Picture Library: 9,13 (David Kay), 26,30 (Ian Griffiths), 10,21
Stock, Boston: 14 (©Steve Hansen);

Library of Congress Cataloging-in-Publication Data: Bailey, Donna. France / Donna Bailey and Anna Sproule. p. cm.—(Where we live) SUMMARY: A young girl describes daily life, sailing and fishing, traditional costumes, housing, customs, food, people, and festivals in Brittany, France. ISBN 0-8114-2561-4 1. Brittany (France)—Social life and customs—Juvenile literature. [1. Brittany (France)—Social life and customs. I. Sproule, Anna. II. Title. III. Series: Bailey, Donna. Where we live. DC611.B851B35 1990 944'.1—dc20 90-9647 CIP AC

2 3 4 5 6 7 8 9 0   LB   96 95 94 93 92 91